TEA

Rhoda Nottridge

Illustrations by John Yates

Food

Apples
Beans and pulses
Bread
Butter
Cakes and biscuits
Cheese
Citrus fruit
Eggs
Fish
Herbs and spices
Meat
Milk
Pasta
Potatoes
Rice
Sugar
Tea
Vegetables

All words that appear in **bold** are explained in the glossary on page 30.

Editors: Roger Coote and Deborah Elliott
First published in 1990 by Wayland (Publishers) Limited
61 Western Road, Hove, East Sussex BN3 1JD, England

British Library Cataloguing in Publication Data
Nottridge, Rhoda
Tea
1. Great Britain. Tea. Social aspects
I. Title II. Yates, John
394.12
ISBN 1 85210 926 2

Typeset by Kalligraphic Design Ltd, Horley, Surrey
Printed in Italy by G. Canale & C.S.p.A., Turin
Bound by Casterman S.A., Belgium

Contents

A cup of tea

There are many different kinds of tea. The type we drink the most is called black tea. It is usually drunk with milk or lemon. Another type is green tea, which is often drunk on its own or with mint. There are also herbal teas, made from plants like peppermint or camomile.

When did people first start to **brew** tea? There are many legends attached to the beginnings of tea drinking. One Chinese legend is that tea was first discovered by an emperor called Shen Nung, who lived around 2,750BC. He was boiling his drinking water when some leaves from an overhanging branch fell into his pot. Interested by the unusual smell that arose from the brewing leaves, he took a taste. He had, perhaps, drunk the first cup of tea in the world.

How tea grows

Tea-leaves grow on an evergreen tree called the camellia, which comes from China. The trees can grow up to 9 m tall. To make the leaves easier to pick, the trees are **pruned** so that they grow into bushes. They need a **tropical** climate with plenty of sun and rain to grow well.

Above *A camellia tree.*

Left *A tea-leaf.*

New bushes are grown from seeds or **cuttings** taken from other bushes. The bushes start to produce good tea-leaves when they are between three and five years old. The young shoots on the tea bushes are then plucked by hand. Only the top two leaves and the bud are picked, because they are young and soft and make the best tea. New leaves appear quickly during the growing season, so the bushes are plucked every week or fortnight. A skilled plucker can gather 35 kg of leaves in a day – enough to make 3,500 cups of tea.

Tea pickers at work on a tea plantation in China. A skilled tea plucker can pick enough leaves in one day to make 3,500 cups of tea!

This flow chart shows how tea leaves are prepared for use in a pot of tea.

The tea factory

The leaves that have been so carefully picked are still not ready to be used to make a pot of tea. They must first go to the tea factory.

Two different types of tea are made at the factory – green tea and black tea. For both types of tea, the leaves are spread on racks and dried with warm air. The leaves soon become withered and limp. They are then

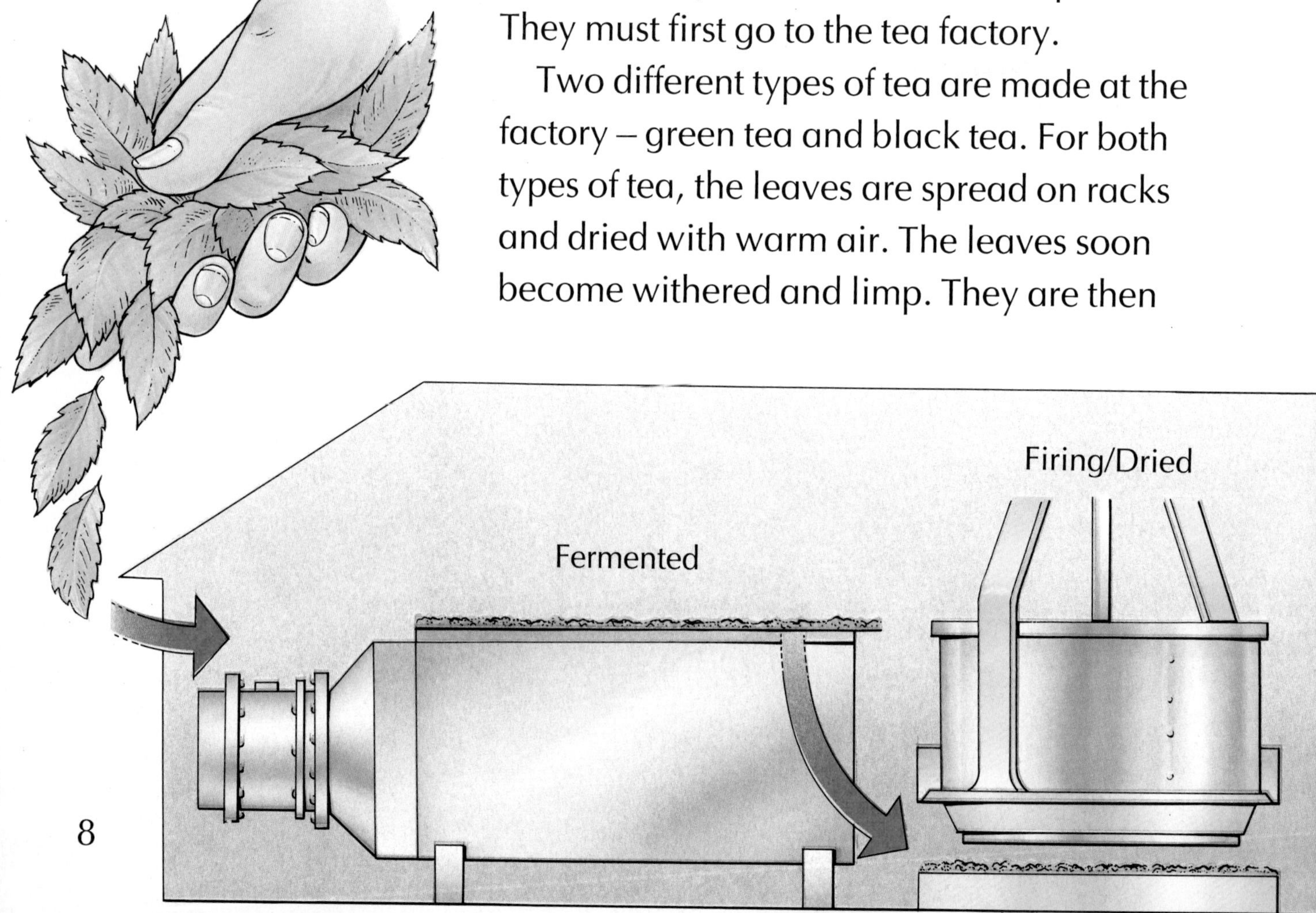

crushed by machines that roll, cut, tear or curl the leaves.

To make black tea, the crushed leaves are then **fermented**. As they ferment the leaves turn a dull, coppery colour and the juices form a dark, sticky liquid on the surface. The leaves are then dried by hot air, which blackens them. The leaves will not be made wet again until they are mixed with boiling water in a teapot. Then all the dried juices will ooze out again, creating the familiar taste and colour of tea.

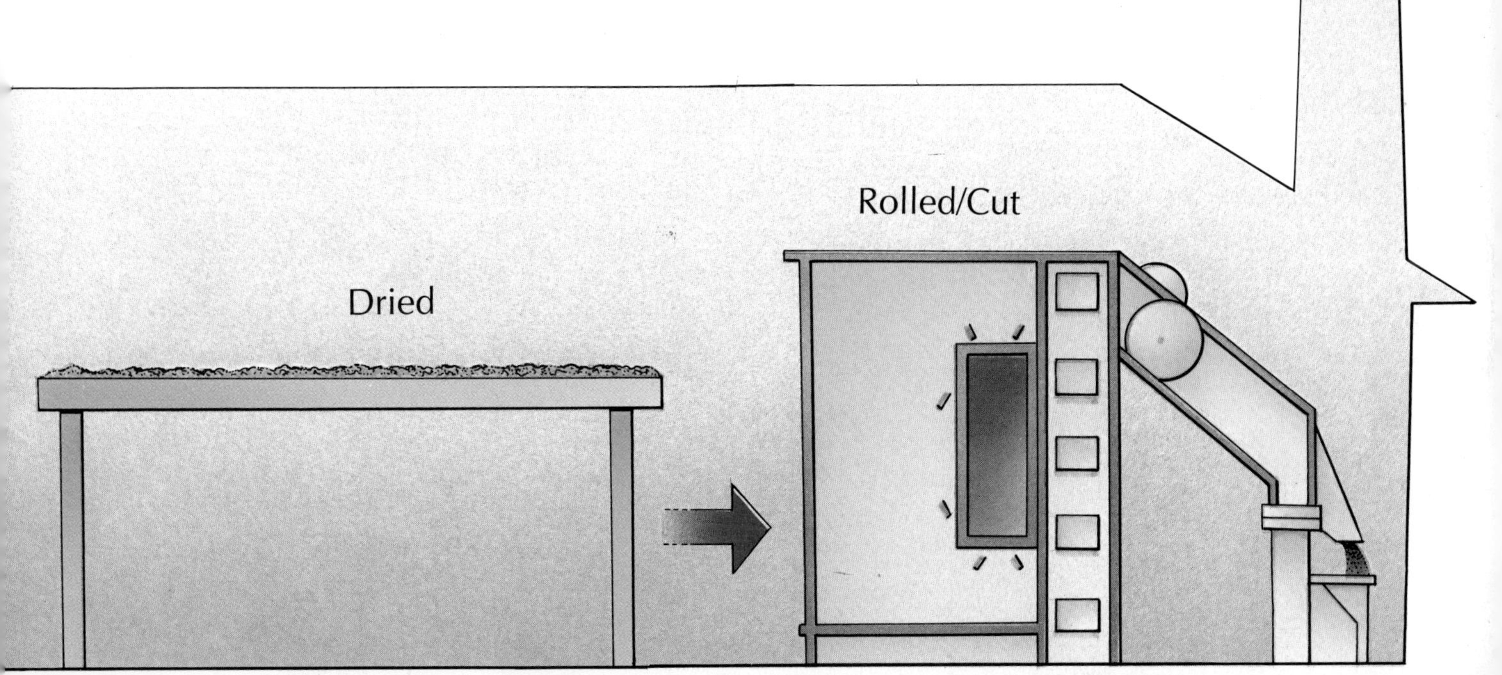

Different types of tea

Refreshing green tea being sold at a tea-shop in Tokyo, Japan.

Green tea is still the favourite type of tea in China, where tea plants first grew. It has a more bitter taste than black tea. When they have been dried in the factory, leaves for green tea are **scalded** with hot steam by machines before they are crushed. This stops them fermenting and turning black. Oolong tea is a mixture of green and black tea which comes from Taiwan.

Tea is not only used as a drink. In Myanmar (or Burma, as it used to be known) the leaves are steamed and left for several months in pits lined with bamboo canes. The leaves are then eaten.

In Tibet, tea-leaves are squashed into a kind of brick. A piece is chipped off into cold water and boiled for an hour until the water is black. Salt, soda and yak butter are stirred in and it is drunk like a soup, with balls of ground barley.

A bowl of black Chinese tea. Hot water is added to make a cup of tea.

Blending tea

There are around 1,500 different types of tea. The different tastes of tea depend on all kinds of things, such as the soil the tea bush grows in and the climate.

At the tea factory the tea is graded into different types by machines that separate the large and small fragments. The smallest pieces of tea, mostly dust, are used to fill tea-bags. The sorted tea is then packed into big plywood boxes

A machine being used to grade tea into different types in Mauritius.

Left *The tea-leaves are packed into boxes.*

Below *Tasting tea in Calcutta.*

lined with foil, called tea-chests. It is ready to be sold at a tea **auction**, either in that country or abroad.

The tea is bought by tea blenders. They are expert tea tasters who sample teas from different growers and make recipes to mix teas that will taste good. For example, Sri Lankan and South Indian teas are good for flavour, African teas have an attractive colour and North Indian teas are strong. Tea blenders may mix as many as 30 different teas to make a blend that tastes, smells and looks good.

The history of tea

As we have seen, tea drinking probably began in China almost 5,000 years ago. It has certainly played an important part in the everyday lives of Chinese and Japanese people for many hundreds of years.

Tea did not reach Europe until about 1610,

An illustration of an early twentieth century Japanese tea ceremony.

when Dutch trading companies brought it back from the East. It became fashionable as a drink for rich people, who paid huge sums for it. Not everyone knew how to drink it. One Duchess is said to have boiled up a brew, thrown away the liquid and tried to eat the soggy tea-leaves.

In the second half of the seventeenth century, coffee houses in London did a roaring trade serving tea. King Charles II tried to stop the sale of tea, coffee, sherbet and chocolate because he thought that the coffee houses were used by people plotting against him. People were so annoyed by this that he pretended to forget about his new law.

Taxes were soon raised on tea, firstly on all places selling it and then on traders bringing it into Britain. As a result, smugglers brought tea into the country secretly to avoid paying taxes. More than 3,000 tonnes of tea were smuggled into the country each year.

This illustration shows a tea-seller at a country railway station in the USSR.

The Boston Tea Party

Pouring tea into Boston harbour.

In 1773 tea was almost as popular in North America as it was in Europe. Many taxes on imports from Britain to America had been stopped, because the American colonies objected to paying taxes to Britain. However, the British decided to keep a tax of a penny on every pound (454 grams) of tea.

Americans were furious and decided that they would stop drinking tea rather than pay taxes to a country that had no right to profit from them.

On 16 December 1773, a British ship arrived at Boston harbour bringing a cargo of tea. About 90 men, dressed as Indians, boarded the ship, burst open the tea-chests and threw the contents into the harbour. Encouraged by cheers from the shore, the men boarded two more tea-carrying ships and ruined their cargoes too. The protest

was well organized and nobody was hurt.

The Boston Tea Party, as it became known, captured the independent spirit of the Americans. They began drinking more coffee in preference to tea, and destroyed or refused landing to tea cargoes in all American ports. The Tea Party started demonstrations that led to the American War of Independence, from which the USA was formed. Even today, coffee is much more popular than tea in the USA.

On 16 December 1773, 90 Americans destroyed the tea cargoes on British ships in Boston harbour. The 'Boston Tea Party' was an American protest at having to pay taxes to Britain.

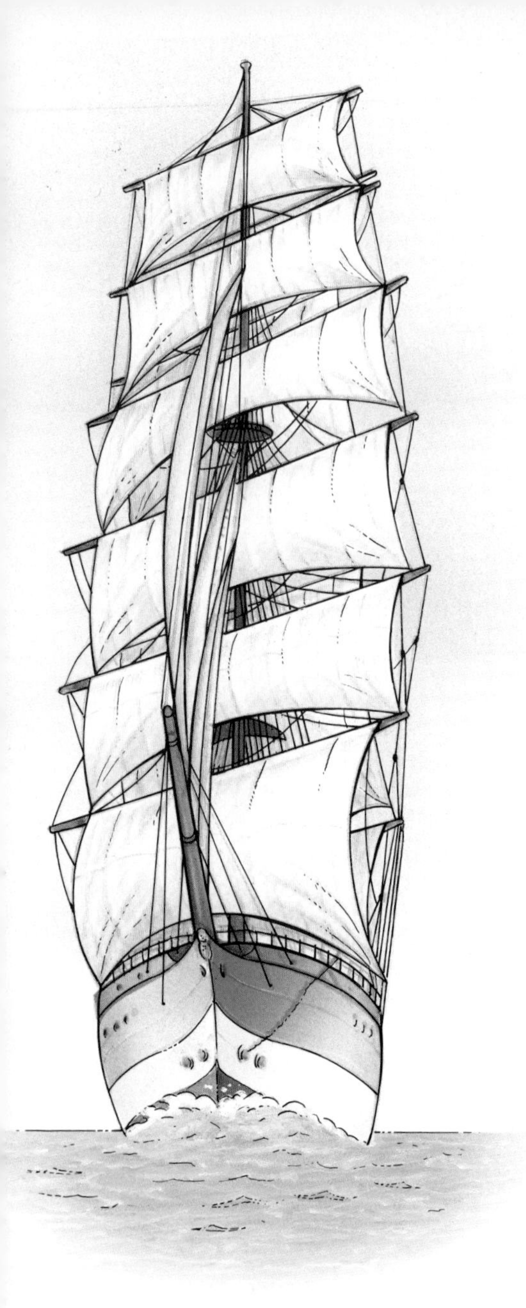

Tea clippers

In the early years of the nineteenth century, bringing tea to the tables of Europeans and Americans involved a slow and dangerous journey by sea. Boats from China took six months to reach Europe. The slow-moving ships were constantly in danger from stormy seas and pirates.

In 1812 the American war with Britain helped to create a new kind of tea boat. The British ships outnumbered the American ones, so the Americans developed a faster, smaller boat. It had huge sails and could outrun the slow British ships. The Americans then used their new design to build faster tea-carrying ships, called clippers. They cut the sailing time from China by half with a clipper called the *Rainbow*. The British later followed their example and built clippers of their

A painting of the American tea clipper, the 'Antarctica'.

own. The fastest tea clipper was the American-built *Lightning*, which travelled almost as fast as a modern ocean liner.

Rivalry over the speed of tea clippers caught the interest of the British public. They waited with excitement to see which clipper would make the fastest journey from China. This became an annual race in which 100 British tea clippers sailed from Shanghai to London.

The tea trade today

Above *Early morning tea drinkers in Hong Kong.*

India is now the largest grower of tea in the world, followed by China and Sri Lanka. Tea is also grown in other parts of Asia, the USSR, South America, Africa and the Middle East. Every year around 2 million tonnes of tea are produced.

To cope with the demand for tea, areas of rainforest have been cut down and the land has been replanted with tea bushes. This creates a

Right *Part of the Brazilian rainforest that has been cut down.*

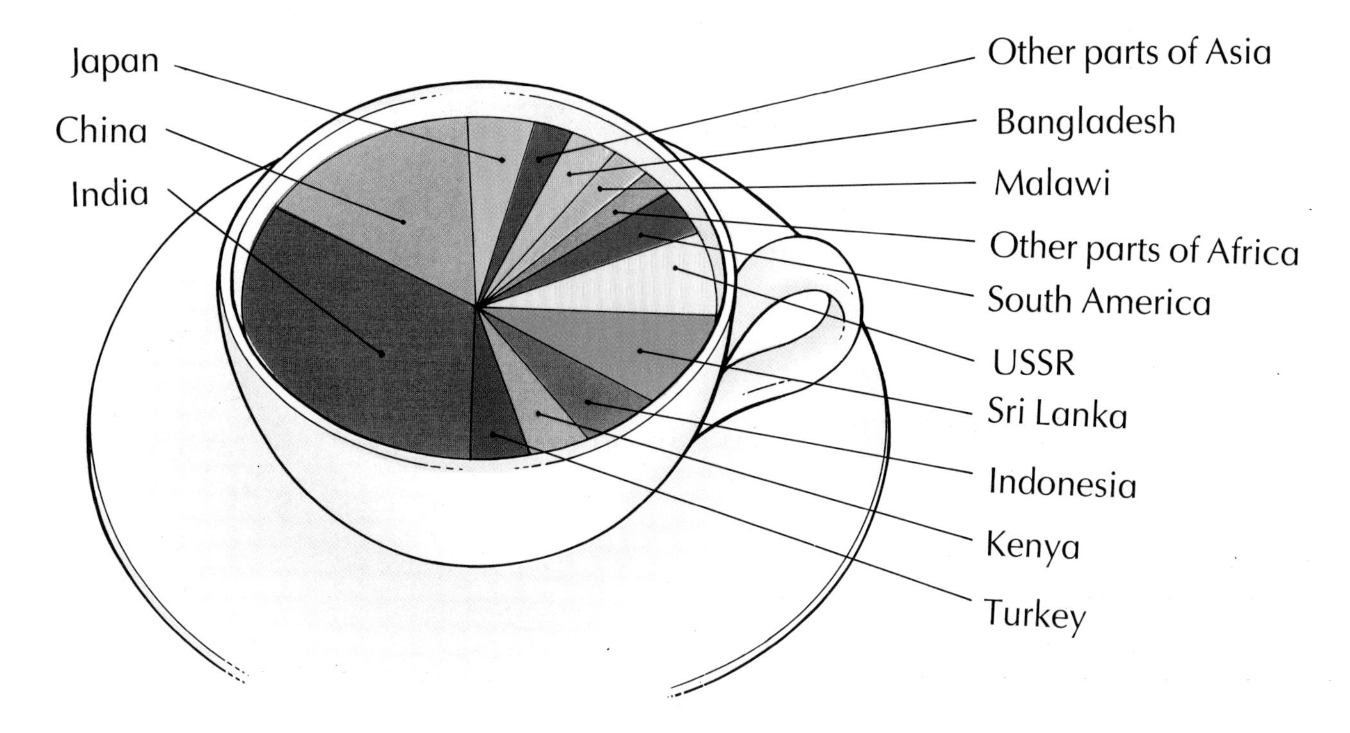

The amounts of tea grown in certain countries.

problem because the world's rainforests help to produce the oxygen that we need to breathe. But many poor countries need the money that they get from growing tea, so rainforests continue to be chopped down.

Britain imports more tea than any other country and drinks a quarter of all the tea produced in the world. Irish and British adults drink, on average, three cups of tea every day.

Drinking tea

Tea is important as a social drink. Offering someone a cup of tea is a way of being friendly. In the USSR people sweeten their tea with jam and in the USA they drink it cold, but wherever it is drunk tea serves a social purpose.

In Japan drinking tea is sometimes part of an important **ceremony**. The idea for the ceremony began over 1,000 years ago, when **Buddhist** monks used to drink tea together.

It is a great honour to be invited to a Japanese tea ceremony. The guests first wait in the garden outside the tea house. They then move into a small room where a light meal is served. After the meal the tea set is brought in. The guests relax and listen to the sound of the tea brewing. The tea is then passed around the guests in a bowl which they all drink from. It is a kind of

A tea-drinking ceremony in Casablanca.

Tea ceremonies are an important part of Japanese culture.

green tea which has been whipped up so that it is frothy.

The Japanese tea ceremony is a way of helping the guests to concentrate on the beauty and simplicity of everything around them. It has become a famous part of Japanese life and is still performed today.

Tea and your body

For many years tea was thought of as a medicine as well as a drink. In fact at first it was sold only in chemists' shops called apothecaries. In the 1700s a Dutchman called Dr Bontekoe thought that it was quite reasonable to drink as many as 200 cups a day.

Tea helps the body's digestion to work. Another reason why people like to drink tea is that it contains a substance called **caffeine**. In

A sheep rancher making tea, known as 'boiling the billy', in the Australian outback.

Left *Iced tea is a popular drink in the USA.*

Below *Mid-morning tea in Algeria.*

small amounts caffeine gives people a temporary feeling of being more awake. This is why people often drink tea when they get up in the morning. However, Dr Bontekoe was wrong to suggest that it is healthy to drink 200 cups of tea in a day. If you drink too much tea the caffeine can make you feel shaky and ill.

If you drink your tea without sugar, it is much healthier than drinking a can of cola, which contains a lot of sugar. Tea is not good for young children. For older people tea is a pleasant drink that is not harmful to the body, as long as it is not taken in large quantities.

Make sure there is an adult around when you make tea.

Making tea

Tea can be made in many ways. This is a traditional way to make a good cup of tea.

You will need:
a kettle
water
a good blend of tea
(either loose or tea-bags)
sugar
milk or lemon
a teapot
a tea strainer (if you are
using loose tea)
cups and saucers
a sugar bowl
a milk jug

1. Prepare a tea tray with cups, saucers, teaspoons, a jug of milk or some slices of lemon, and a bowl of sugar (if anyone takes sugar).

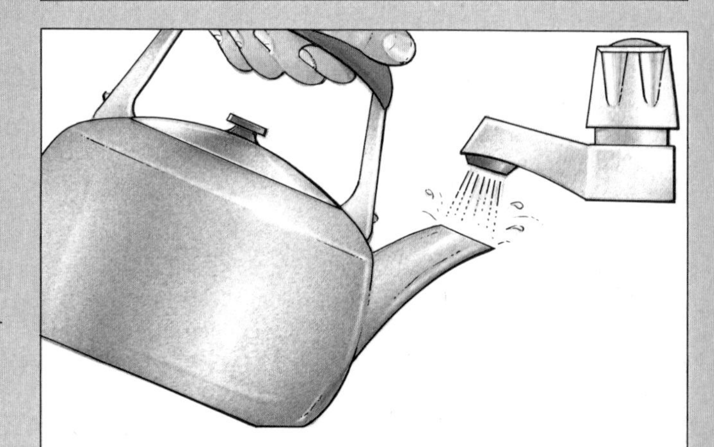

2. Fill the kettle with fresh water from the cold tap.

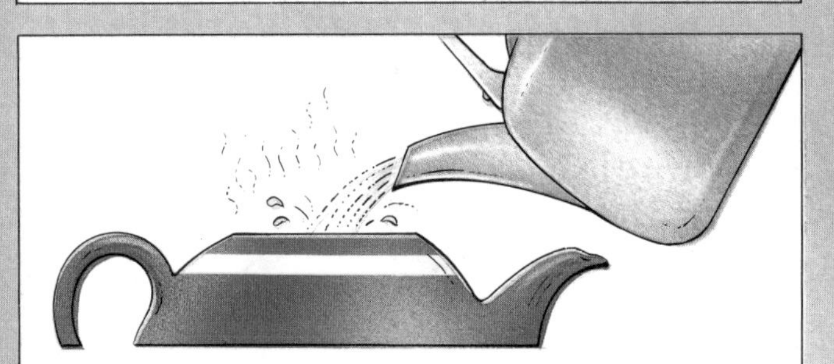

3. When the water in the kettle is warm, but before it boils, carefully pour a little water into the teapot to warm it. Put the kettle back to boil. When the teapot feels warm to the touch on the outside, pour away the water in it down the sink.

4. Now put some tea into the empty teapot. Put in one teaspoon or tea-bag for each person having tea and then add one extra 'for the pot'.

5. When the kettle has boiled, very carefully pour the water into the teapot. Put the lid on the teapot and leave the tea to brew for five minutes. Put a tea-cosy on the pot if you have one.

6. When it is ready, stir the tea briefly. Pour the tea into the cups, using a tea strainer if you have used loose tea. Add milk or lemon and sugar if required.

Iced tea

Iced tea was invented in 1904 by an American who was trying to sell tea at a trade fair in St Louis, USA. The weather was so warm that no one wanted to drink his hot tea, so he put some ice cubes in a glass and poured tea over them.

To make iced tea you will need:
3 tea-bags
500ml of fresh, cold water
ice cubes (if available)
a large jug and glasses

1. Put the tea-bags into the jug with the cold water.
Leave for at least three hours, or overnight if possible.

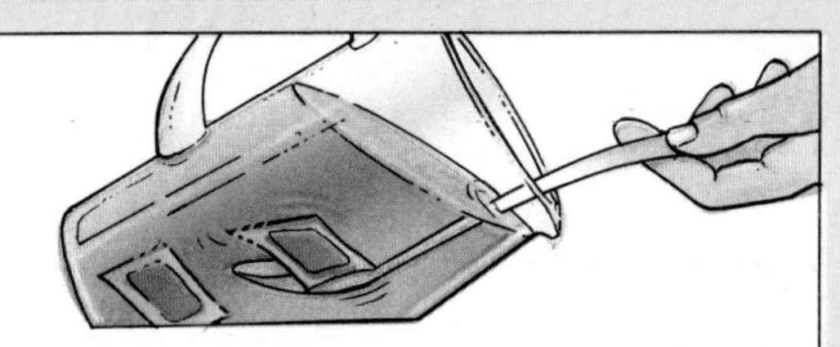

2. Take out the tea-bags and throw them away.

3. Leave the tea in the refrigerator until it is chilled.

4. Put some ice cubes in glasses and pour the tea over them.

To make iced lemon tea, add 100ml of lemon juice to the tea before pouring out. Serve with sugar and slices of lemon to taste.

Apple tea

You will need:

500ml iced tea
500ml sparkling apple juice
sugar to taste
ice cubes (if available)
100ml lemon juice
1 apple

1. Mix the iced tea, apple juice and lemon juice together in the jug.

2. Taste the mixture and add a couple of teaspoons of sugar if you think it needs to taste sweeter. Stir in a little at a time until it dissolves.

3. Cut the apple into slices, taking out the pips.

4. Put two slices of apple in each glass with some ice cubes. Pour the liquid into the glasses.

Glossary

Auction A sale where the goods are bought by the person who offers the highest price.

Brew To soak tea-leaves in boiling water to make tea.

Buddhist A person who follows the religion of Buddhism and worships the Buddha.

Caffeine A chemical that makes people feel more lively. It is found in tea, coffee and cocoa.

Ceremony A formal act which is often performed according to traditional rules.

Cuttings Parts which have been cut from a plant (usually leaves or stems) and allowed to grow roots of their own so that they will develop into new plants.

Fermented When a substance has undergone a chemical reaction that has changed it into different substances.

Pruned When parts of a plant are cut off to make the plant grow in a certain way. Tea plants are pruned so that they stay as bushes.

Scalded When something is burned with a hot liquid or with steam.

Taxes Money that people have to pay to their government.

Tropical A word describing the climate in parts of the world where it is hot and sunny with lots of rain.

Books to read

A Cup of Tea by Andrew Langley (Wayland, 1982)
A First Look at Tea by V. Pitt (Franklin Watts, 1982)
Food in History by S. Robertson (Wayland, 1983)
Tea by Michael Smith (Ladybird, 1981)

For older readers:
Beverages by Jacqueline Dineen (Young Library, 1985)
Focus on Tea by Alan Blackwood (Wayland, 1985)

Index

Picture acknowledgements

The photographs in this book were provided by: Mary Evans Picture Library 14, 15, 16, 17, 19; Hutchison Library 7, 10, 11, 13 (bottom), 20 (top), 23, 24, 25 (bottom); Christine Osborne/ Middle East Pictures 13 (top), 22, 25, (top); Peter Stiles COVER; ZEFA Picture Library 12, 20 (bottom).